Handwriting Workbook - Straight
Grade 1
Student Edition

D1534314

create.mheducation.com

ISBN-13: 9780076858996

ISBN-10: 0076858995

Contents

Name _____

Left-Handed Writers

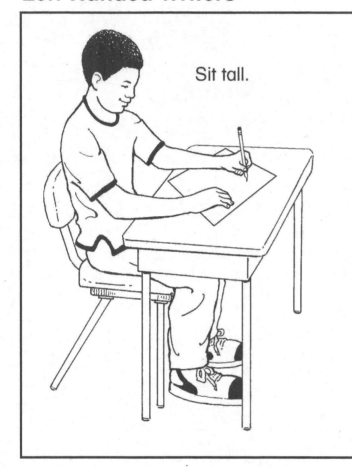

Sit tall.

Look at the picture.
Hold your pencil like this.

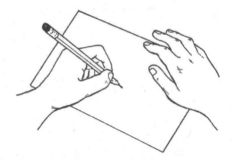

Slant your paper like this.

Name _____

Right-Handed Writers

Look at the picture.
Hold your pencil like this.

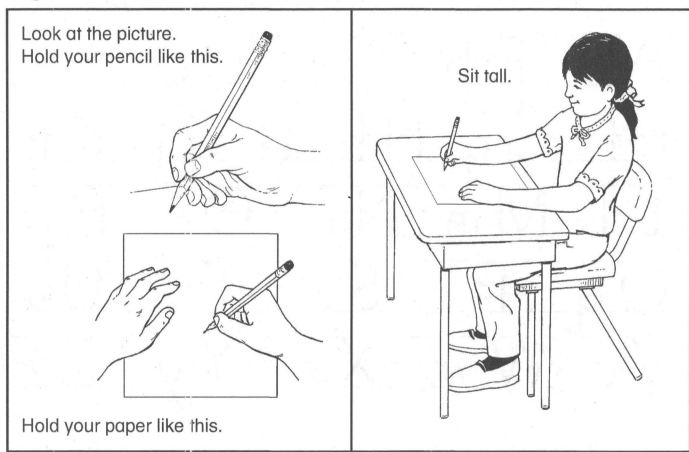

Hold your paper like this.

Sit tall.

Name _____

The Manuscript Alphabet

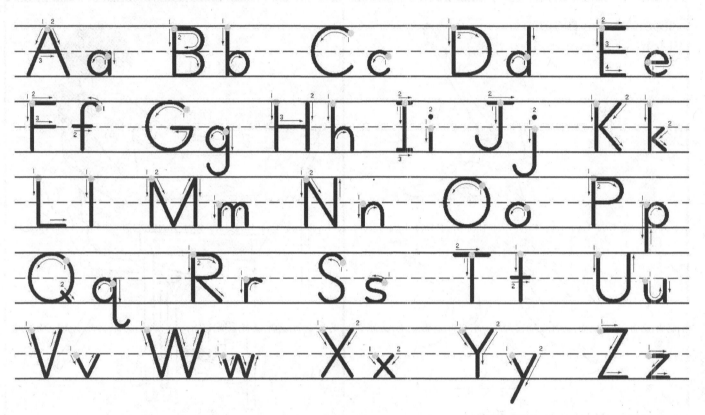

Directions: These are the capital and small letters of the alphabet. The arrows show how to write each letter. Point to each pair of letters and name it. Then trace the letters of your name with your finger.

Name _____

Handwriting Lines

Directions: Where are the ladybugs? Draw a line around the ladybugs on the top line. Color the ladybugs on the middle line orange. Draw an X on the ladybugs on the bottom line.

Name _____

Left to Right

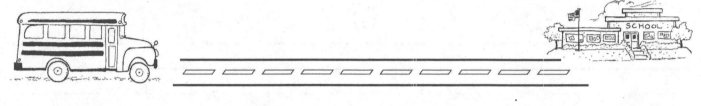

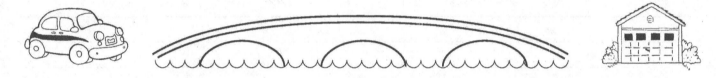

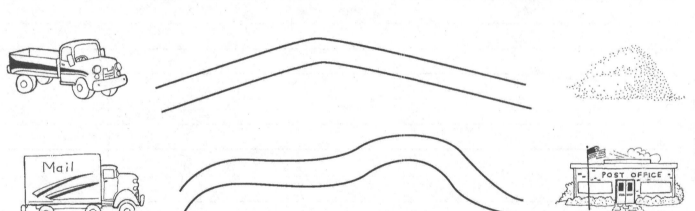

Directions: Where is the school bus going? Draw a line from left to right. Where is the car going? Draw a line from left to right. Complete the page on your own.

Name _____

Straight and Curved Lines

Directions: Trace the lines.

Name _____

I

i

I i

Ivan is in. Ida is in.

Directions: Trace and write I and i.

Name _____

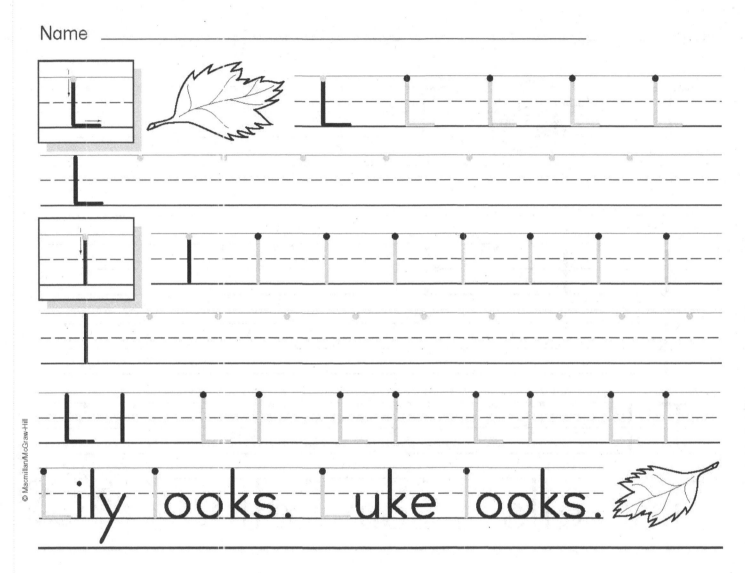

Directions: Trace and write L and l.

Name _____

Tim tells. Tam tells.

Directions: Trace and write T and t.

Name _____

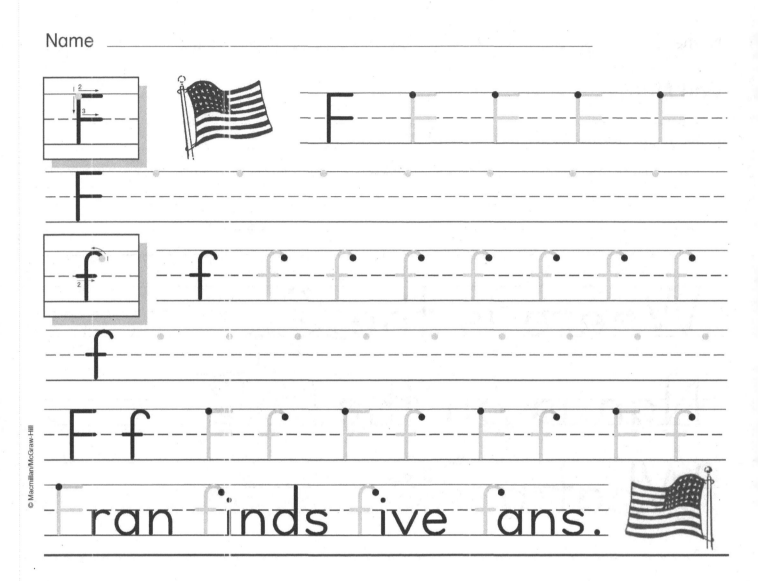

Fran finds five fans.

Directions: Trace and write F and f.

Name _____

End Marks

? ? ? ? ? • • • • •

| | | | |

Where is the 🙂 ?

Nan is on the 🚌

What a 🐕 !

Directions: Trace and write the end marks.

Name _____

Review

Circle your best letters.

I I   i i

L L   l l

T T   t t

F F   f f

Ike   fit   Flora lit

ke   ora

Directions: Trace and write the letters and words.

Name _____

Circles and Part Circles

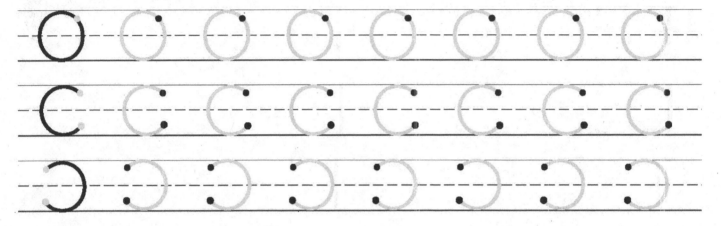

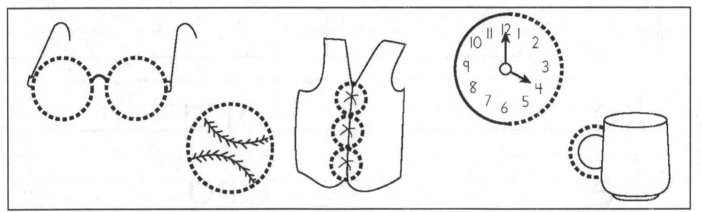

Directions: Trace the lines.

Name _____

Finding Circles in Letters

O	Q	L	Y	O	M
C	X	C	E	G	H
c	r	m	d	l	a
ɔ	b	v	t	k	p
c	s	n	e	g	f
C	K	D	W	D	V

Directions: Trace over the line at the beginning of each row. Then draw a circle around the letter or letters that have that line.

Name _____

O   O   O   O   O   O

O   O   O

o   o   o   o   o   o   o   o   o

o   o   o

off   Omar   on   Oona

ff   mar   n   ona

Directions: Trace and write O and o.

Name _____

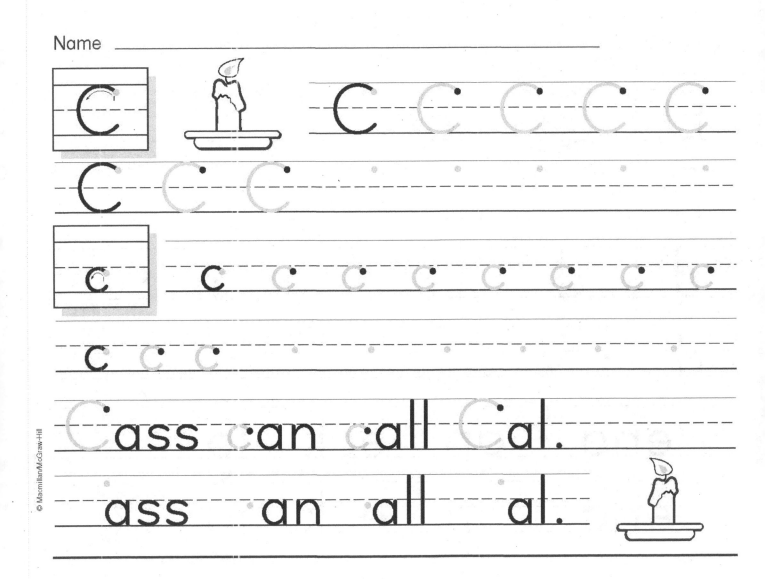

C C C C C C

C C C

c c c c c c c c c c

c c c

Cass can call Cat.

ass an all at.

Directions: Trace and write C and c.

Name _____

D   D   D   D   D   D   D

D   D   D

d   d   d   d   d   d   d   d   d

d   d   d

Dena Dan deck dig

ena   an   eck   ig

Directions: Trace and write D and d.

Name _____

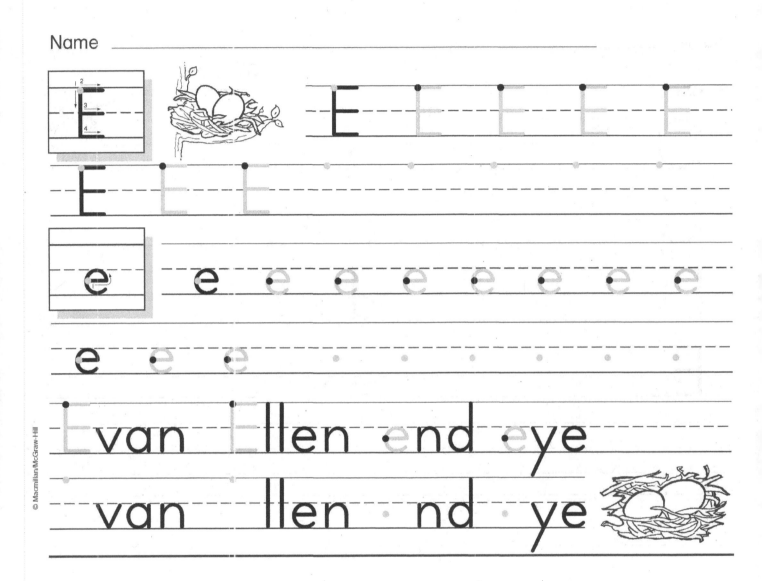

Directions: Trace and write E and e.

Name _____

Review

Circle your best letters.

O O ○   o ○

C C   c c

D D   d d

E E   e e

Otto cold Dad Ellie

Directions: Trace and write the letters. On the last line, trace the words.

Name _____

A Story

| I | let | did | to | Ted |

_ went _ the zoo with ___.

We saw a 🐻. We saw

a 🦭. A 🐒 looked at us.

We _____ have fun.

Please _____ us go again!

Directions: Complete the story. Use words from the box.
Read your story to a friend.

Name _____

Slant Lines

Directions: Trace and copy the lines.

Name _____

A A A A A A A

A A A

a a a a a a a a a

a a a

Alex and Amy

lex nd my

Directions: Trace and write A and a.

Name _____

V V V V V V

V V V V

v v v v v v v v v

v v v v

very Vera van Victor

ery era an ictor

Directions: Trace and write V and v.

Name _____

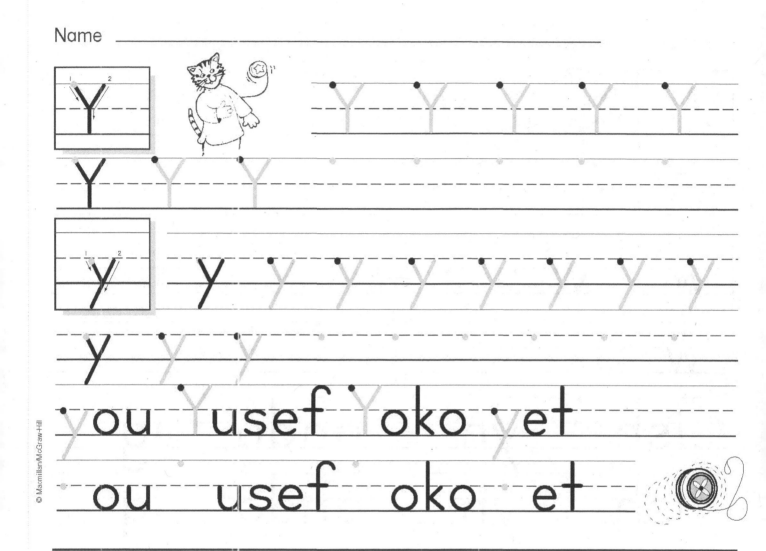

you Yusef Yoko yet

ou usef oko et

Directions: Trace and write Y and y.

Name _____

W   W   W   W   W

W   W   W

w   w   w   w   w   w   w   w

w   w   w

wish   Wyn   Wanda   wig

ish   yn   anda   ig

Directions: Trace and write W and w.

Name _____

N

N N N N N N

N N N

n n n n n n n n n

n n n

Nan naps. Nick naps.

an aps. ick aps.

Directions: Trace and write N and n.

Name _____

Review

Circle your best letters.

A   A   a   a

V   V   v   v

Y   Y   y   y

W   W   w   w

N   N   n   n

Nancy   wave   yell   now

Directions: Trace and write the letters. Then trace and write the words.

Name _____

Directions

First, fold the paper.

in half.

Next, draw.

Last, cut it out.

What did Keisha make?

_____

_____

_____

Directions: Trace the time-order words in the directions.
What did the girl make? Write your answer.

Name _____

Just Right

too close

just right

too far

not like this

like this

Directions: Letters in a word should not be too close. Letters in a word should not be too far apart. Leave the space of a pencil point between letters. Leave the space of a pencil between words.

Name _____

G   G   G   G   G   G

G   G   G

g   g   g   g   g   g   g   g   g

g   g   g

Gus goes. Gina goes.

us oes. ina oes.

Directions: Trace and write G and g.

Name _____

P   P   P   P   P   P   P   P

P   P   P   P

p   p   p   p   p   p   p   p   p   p   p

p   p   p

pot   Pam   Pablo   pup

pot   am   ablo   up

Directions: Trace and write P and p.

Name _____

S

S

s

s

Sari sees. Sam sees.

ari ees. am ees.

Directions: Trace and write S and s.

Name _____

M   M M M M M M

M   M M M

m   m m m m m m m m

m   m m

Min meets Max.

in eets ax.

Directions: Trace and write M and m.

Name _____

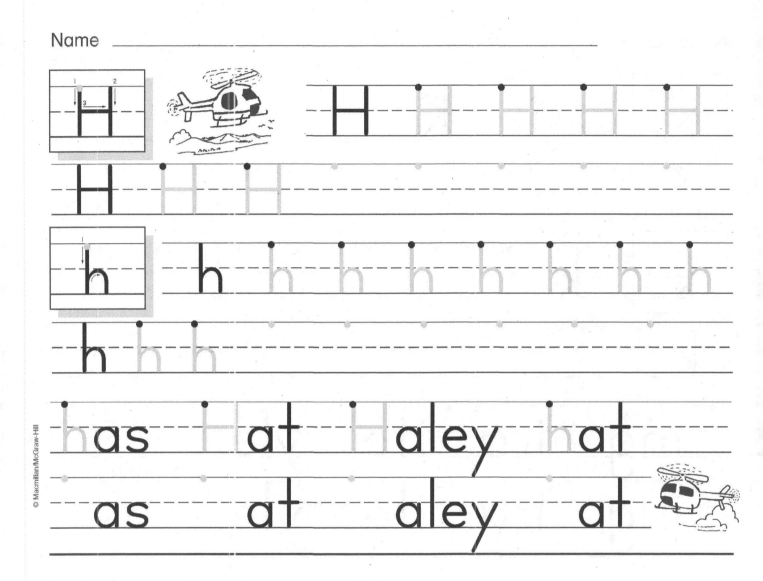

Directions: Trace and write H and h.

Name _____

K K K K K K K

K K K

k k k k k k k k

k k k

King Kira kite Kyle
ing ira ite yle

Directions: Trace and write K and k.

Name _____

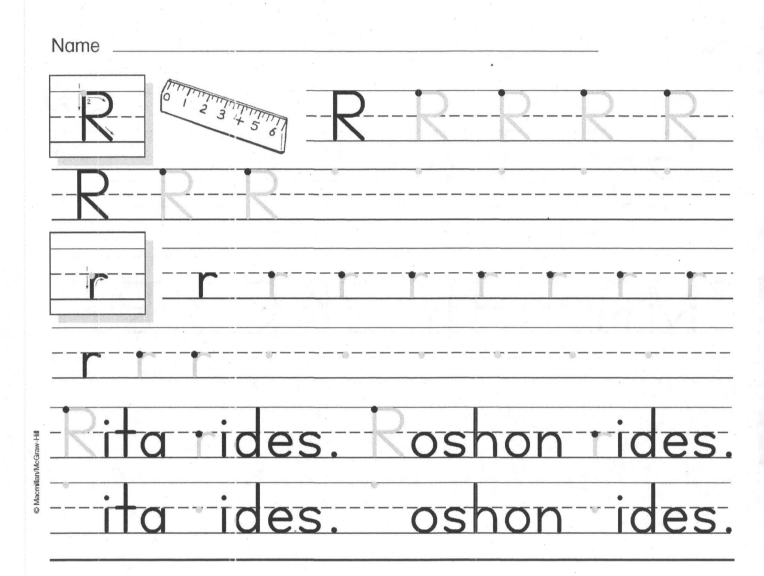

Directions: Trace and write R and r.

Name _____

Review

Circle your best letters.

G g   P p   S s

M m   H h   K k   R r

mop   gap   Maria   Sam

Directions: Trace and write the letters. Trace and write the words.

Name _____

Sentences

Here are two dolls.

One doll can walk.

One doll can talk.

Which one do you like?

Directions: Trace and copy the sentences. Then color the doll you like best. Tell why.

Name _____

Size and Shape

I can Arite.

I can write.

You can read this.

You can read this.

Directions: Look at the first and second rows. Draw a line around the row with the best shaped letters. Then copy the sentence. Look at the next two rows. Which row is easier to read? Draw a line around that row. Then copy the sentence.

Name _____

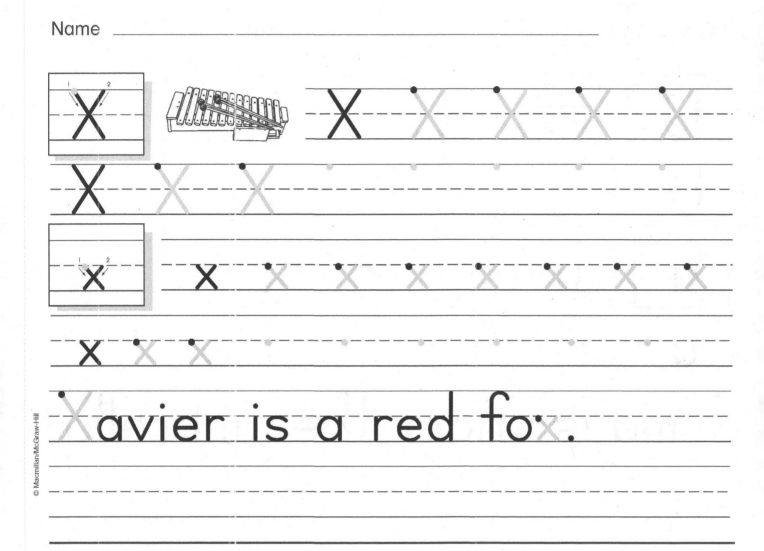

© Macmillan/McGraw-Hill

Directions: Trace and write X and x. Write the sentence.

Name _____

U

U U U U U U

U U U U

u   u u u u u u u u

u u u u

Uma is under the umbrella.

Directions: Trace and write U and u. Write the sentence.

Name _____

Q

Q   Q   Q   Q   Q

Q   Q   Q

q   q   q   q   q   q   q   q

q   q   q

Quin is quick.

Directions: Trace and write Q and q. Write the sentence.

Name _____

Numbers

one 1   one 1

two 2   two 2

three 3   three 3

four 4   four 4

five 5   five 5

Directions: Trace and write the words and the numbers. Then write the numbers 1 through 5 on the last line.

Name _____

More Numbers

six 6   six 6

seven 7   seven 7

eight 8   eight 8

nine 9   nine 9

ten 10   ten 10

Directions: Trace and write the words and the numbers. Then write the numbers 6 through 10 on the last line.

Name _____

A Rhyme

One, two, buckle my shoe.

1   2

Three, four, shut the door.

3   4

Five, six, pick up sticks.

5   6

Directions: Trace the words and the numbers. Then write the numbers 1 through 6 on the lines.

Name _____

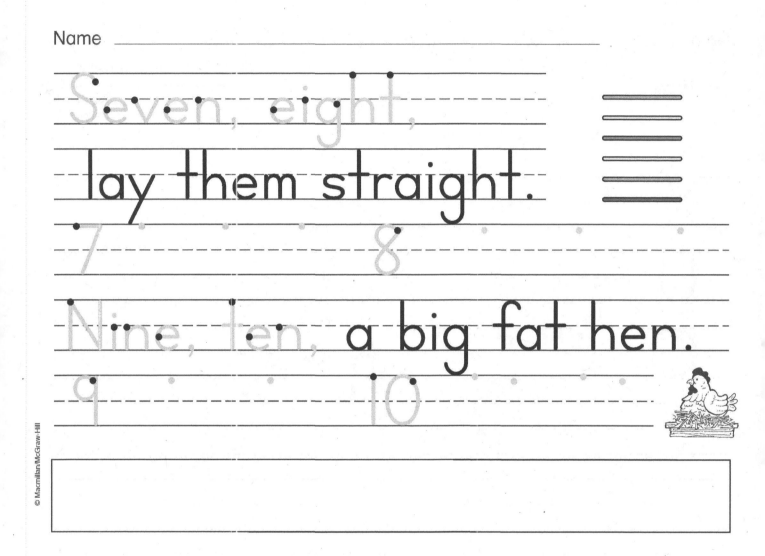

Seven, eight,

lay them straight.

7   8

Nine, ten, a big fat hen.

9   10

Directions: Trace the words and the numbers. Then write the numbers 7 through
10 on the lines. Write a number in the box and draw a picture to show how many.

Name _____

Review

Circle your best letters.

X X   x x

U U   u u

Q Q   q q

The quick fox ran home.

Directions: Trace and write the letters. Then trace and write the words.

Name _____

A Story

Fred is a silly pup.

He hides his bones.

He hides his toys.

Directions: Trace and write the sentences and then read the story. Where is Fred, the dog?
Use the last line to answer.

Name _____

Staying on the Lines

Animals cannot cook.

Animals cannot cook.

Most animals have to hunt for food.

Some animals eat plants.

Directions: Look at the first two rows. Draw a line around the sentence that is sitting on the bottom line. Look at the next sentences. What is wrong? Choose one of the sentences to copy. Watch your margins!

Name _____

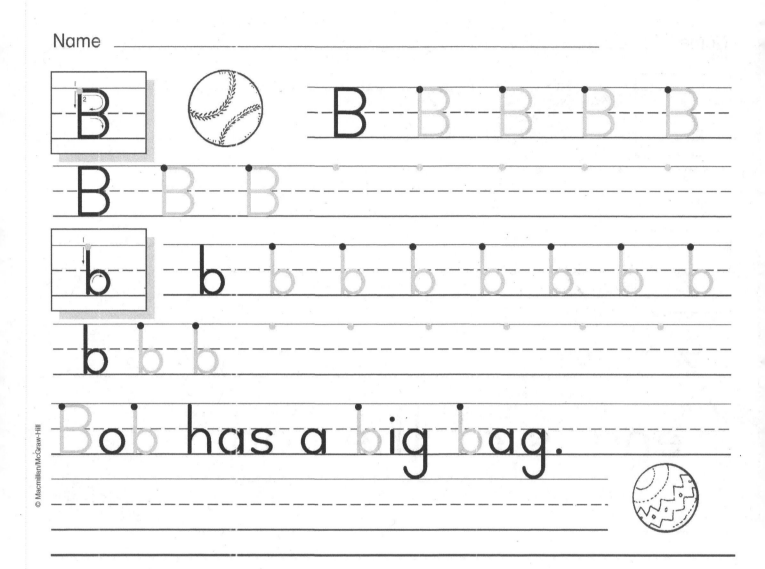

© Macmillan/McGraw-Hill

Directions: Trace and write B and b. Then write the sentence.

Name _____

Z   Z Z Z Z Z Z

Z Z Z Z Z Z Z

z   z z z z z z z z

z z z z z z

Zena is at the zoo.

© Macmillan/McGraw-Hill

Directions: Trace and write Z and z. Then write the sentence.

Name _____

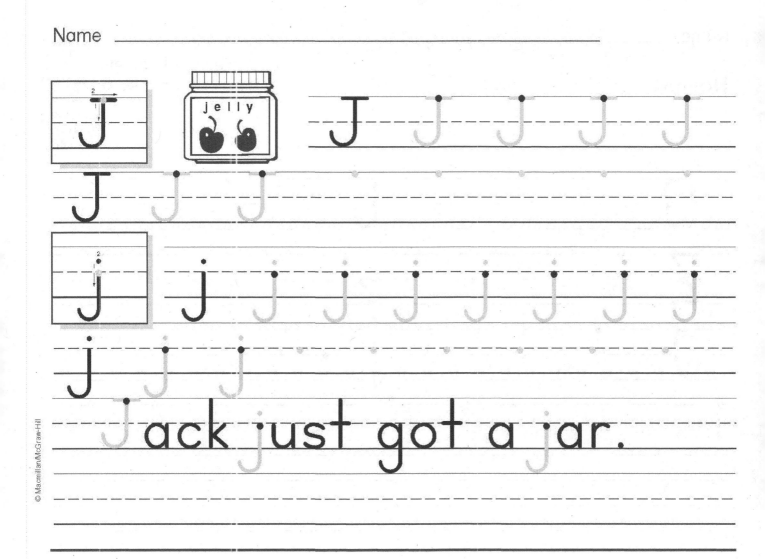

Directions: Trace and write J and j. Then write the sentence.

Name _____

Review

Circle your best letters.

B B B   b b b

Z Z Z   z z z

J J J   j j j
         J J J

Ben saw Julia at the zoo.

Directions: Trace and write the letters. Then write the sentence.

Name _____

A Book Report

My name is _____

Title of My Book _____

_____

I like the book because _____

_____

Directions: Write your full name. Write the title of a book you like.
Then tell why you like the book.

Name _____

Favorite Words

Circle your best word.

mat   likes

saw   one

what   her

there   they

© Macmillan/McGraw-Hill

Directions: Choose words to write on the lines.

Name _____

More Favorite Words

Circle your best word.

pick	two
see	small
no	pan
look	red
this	use

My name is _____

Directions: Choose words to write on the lines. On the last line, write your name.

Name _____

Write a Story

Circle your best word.

Directions: Draw a picture in the box. Write a story about your picture. Use your best handwriting.

Name _____

Days of the Week

Circle your best word.

Monday

Tuesday

Wednesday

Thursday

Friday   Saturday   Sunday

Directions: Write the name of each day.

Name _____

Months of the Year

Circle your best word.

January

February

March

April

May

June

Directions: Write the name of each month.

Name _____

Circle your best word.

July

August

September

October

November

December

Directions: Write the name of each month.

Name _____